Wall Hangings of Today

Vera Sherman

WALL HANGINGS OF TODAY

Mills & Boon Limited, London

Charles T. Branford Co., USA

First published in Great Britain
1972 by Mills & Boon Ltd
17–19 Foley Street, London WIA IDR

U.S. edition 1972 by
Charles T. Branford Company
Newton Centre, Massachusetts 02159

ISBN 0 263 51729 2

American ISBN 1 8231 5037 2

LCCCN 75–182362

Printed in Great Britain
by Ebenezer Baylis & Son Ltd
The Trinity Press, Worcester
and London

Contents

*Note: within the categories, works
are listed in alphabetical order of
artist's name.*

Acknowledgements

Many people have helped and encouraged me in all aspects associated with the 'Contemporary Hangings'. To them and to those who have helped in the preparation of this book I am greatly indebted. In particular I would like to thank

Mark Gerson, F.I.I.P., for the colour photography and almost all the black and white photographs.

Robert St. George Sproule for the preparation of almost all the blocks.

The Embroiderers' Guild and the Editor of *Embroidery* for the loan of the blocks used on pages 30, 31, 32, 43, 44, 45, 62.

The Editor of *Creative Needlecraft* for the loan of the block used on page 56.

The many private collectors and public authorities who have allowed works from the 'Contemporary Hangings' now in their collections to be reproduced.

The artists for permission to reproduce their works.

Mrs. Joan Bryant for her interest, enthusiasm and support.

Preface

This book is the direct outcome of the interest created by a series of touring exhibitions entitled 'Contemporary Hangings' which it has been my privilege to organize and present.

The first collection of 'Contemporary Hangings' was shown during June 1965 and it quickly became apparent there was a great need for this type of exhibition, embracing as it did the work of distinguished artist-craftsmen specializing in Batik, Collage, Embroidery, Tapestry and Tie and Dye, many of the crafts being then little known to the general public. Later collections were to include other weaving forms and allied crafts such as Macramé.

The enthusiasm with which the first exhibition was received and the many requests for it to be shown elsewhere resulted in a tour being arranged. Over a period of two years the collection was shown in thirty of the principal Art Galleries in the United Kingdom and Ireland. Recorded attendance figures exceeded 100,000.

Following repeated requests the Second, Third, Fourth and Fifth Contemporary Hangings were assembled and to date over half a million visitors have attended 175 showings. In addition collections concentrating on a particular medium have been arranged for Colleges and schools. Small collections of 'Contemporary Pictures in Fabric and Thread' have been made available to centres with limited space, and exhibitions arranged for specific occasions.

In the summer of 1970 the Twentieth King's Lynn Festival of Music and the Arts was held under the patronage of Her Majesty the Queen Mother. Having the honour of organizing an exhibition to be held in the Priory Church of Saint Margaret during the Festival I made a point of including contemporary ecclesiastical hangings.

The exhibition was as enthusiastically received as had been the earlier collections and it is in answer to the continuing requests for information about the exhibits, the artists participating, and the methods and materials they use, that this book is being presented.

The artist-craftsmen of today are versatile and uninhibited. Those represented in the 'Contemporary Hangings' have a background of painting, sculpture and printmaking. They have expert knowledge of a wide range of crafts involving the use of materials such as stained glass, metal and wood. Experienced in many techniques, they have nevertheless found fabric and thread a compelling form of creative expression. It is a medium in which they continue to explore and experiment. Respecting traditional methods, they obey no rules, conforming only to their own self-imposed discipline.

This is not a technical book. It is catalogued only loosely as to media. The works are grouped as to secular and ecclesiastical themes. It is a volume between the covers of which you will find over 100 illustrations of items in the several 'Contemporary Hangings' exhibitions.

I hope you will find the illustrations and accompanying text interesting and enlightening—an introduction to an exciting art form, as well as a permanent record of works you may have seen.

To the artists mentioned here who have so willingly and continuously given me their support I extend my grateful thanks. I hope I have been able to convey to the reader something of the originality and excellence of their work. In this mechanical and automated age we are indebted to the dedicated artists pursuing their time-absorbing crafts. Life is richer for their endeavours.

Vera Sherman

Part 1—Secular

Setting Sun/by Eirian Short   *Appliqué and Embroidery*

Simple appliqué has been used by
Eirian Short for the 5 by 3 feet panel
'Setting Sun'. It is a work vibrant with
colour. The lower part of the satin
background is deep royal blue, the top
section bright yellow. The reflected
sun shape is deep red. The applied
fabrics are machined down with zigzag
stitch and overlaid with a mixture of
embroidery threads including cottons,
synthetic chenille and rayon.

Details of other work by this artist are
to be found on pages 29, 50–51, 64–66
and 97.

Light/by Beryl Ash

Beryl Ash works in a form of batik using flour paste spread on the cloth to resist the dye. Soledon or Procion colours are used. It is a similar method to that employed by the Yoruba people of Nigeria who commonly use indigo as a dye with their starch resists. 'Light' is in yellows and pinks. It is one of a series of panels based on four large circular shapes, all in different combinations of yellows, pinks and reds. Each one is developed in a slightly different way, using only the circle or part of the circle to extend the design. The artist is developing the idea of a central force working outwards, sometimes enclosed, sometimes extending beyond the apparent boundary.

Match/Spring Cycle/by Noel Dyrenforth

Batik

'Match' is an early work by Noel Dyrenforth from the Second Contemporary Hangings. 'Spring Cycle' was produced later and is from the Fourth Contemporary Hangings.

Batik is a process of resist dyeing. Noel Dyrenforth has used molten wax as the resist for the two works illustrated. The molten wax is drawn or painted on to the fabric and in turn dyed, the colour only being accepted by the exposed areas. To achieve more intricacy with further combinations and overlays of colour, the waxing and dyeing process is repeated. Finally the wax is removed to reveal the total effect.

Noel Dyrenforth sets up arresting, clear shapes in juxtaposition with organic elements, conflicting though never assertive. This expression is echoed in the fragmentary effect of the technique. It is caused by the dye infiltrating the cracks in the wax surface, quite spontaneously.

In his approach to his work the artist comments: 'The batik process has a distinctive nature, an unnerving determination; these qualities are a built-in risk to the artist. They seduce, with the result that his autonomy is likely to be forfeited. Once aware of these inherent peculiarities, however, some objectives can be realized that

MATCH

extend beyond a pretty headscarf or tasteful wall hanging. The potential of the wax resist method to express vital concepts is particularly challenging therefore; especially when art, no longer stratified by "fine" and "craft", is becoming more fluid, interacting with the environment.'

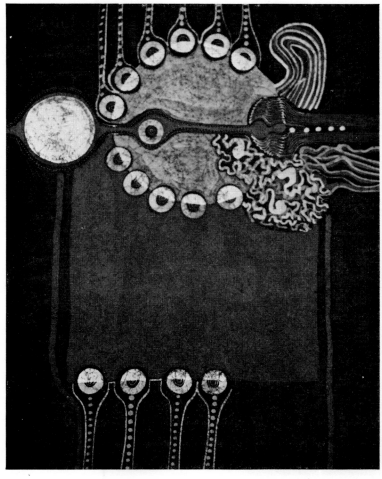

SPRING CYCLE

Cosmic Spring/Coral Symphony/Distant Forces
by Gabriel Sitkey
Batik

When Gabriel Sitkey first turned to batik he was much affected by the discovery that with this technique he could do anything he wished with lines, textures and colour. He observed that lines could have a power beyond the creator, or that he could control them at will. He could make shapes with or without boundaries, create forms in a 'hard edge' manner and texture with a magical quality. Nowadays he is concerned to put more 'light' into his batiks. Radiating pure colours are organized in relation to each other. With dramatic action multitudinous detail occurs which is reminiscent of nature and the organic world. Boundaries become fluid space which is conceived as a countless succession of spatial relationships. These qualities are clearly demonstrated in 'Cosmic Spring', 'Coral Symphony' and 'Distant Forces'.

COSMIC SPRING

CORAL
SYMPHONY

DISTANT
FORCES

Captive Butterfly/by Ellen Beutlich   *Collage*

'Captive Butterfly' is styled collage. In fact many mixed media are incorporated. Ellen Beutlich, wife of the weaver Tadek Beutlich, has easy access to many of the yarns and threads used by her husband. Her interest is to create three-dimensional effects using any technique, fabric or yarn which will achieve this. She experiments with knitting and crochet, combining these with collage.

In 'Captive Butterfly' Ellen Beutlich uses natural sisal and coarsely knitted snarl for the 'net' effect. The butterfly shape is composed of felt and zigzag machine embroidery. The flowers and grasses are made up of gimp, hand spun wool, Fresca embroidery yarn, snarl and slub. Felt and organdie are applied. There is machine satin stitch in places but for the most part hand stitchery is used and a very free effect created.

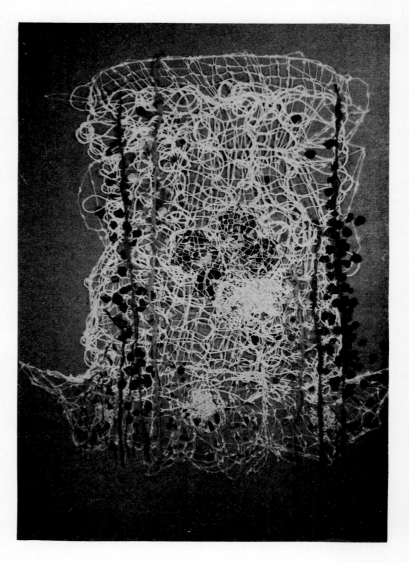

Wotan Calling Erda/*by Richard Box*   *Collage*

'Wotan calling Erda' is from the first series of collage works contributed by Richard Box to the 'Contemporary Hangings'. It was a series in which he aimed at recreating the atmosphere of Wagner's music of the Ring cycle.

It was through colour and texture that Richard Box sought to produce atmosphere. Purple, dark brown and black predominate and the arrangement of fabric and fur convey the emergence of Erda from the sinister depths of her cave.

At the time the work was executed the artist took colour and texture as first priorities, overall drawing and structure being then of secondary importance.

He was aware that form and shape and their cohesion into design and composition were important but did not consider them as crucial as he does now.

Today whilst recognizing that textural qualities and arrangements of one colour against another are important, he feels they would have worked better if they had been contained in a more interesting composition.

'If drawing is the spirit and the colour of the senses you must first draw to cultivate the spirit and to be able to lead colour into spiritual parts.'

—Matisse.

An ecclesiastical panel by Richard Box is illustrated on page 94.

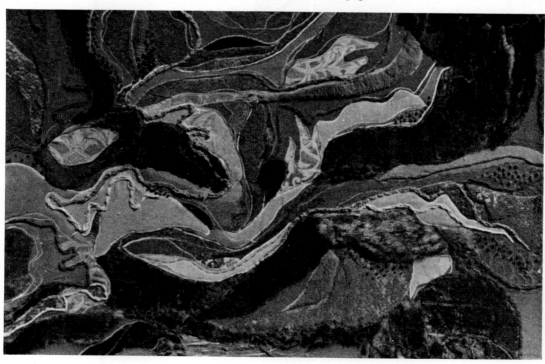

Silver Movement/by Jennifer Gray   *Collage*

Jennifer Gray's work is frequently listed as embroidery or collage but it does not easily fall into either of these categories. She is primarily concerned with the reflective qualities of fabric. In 'Silver Movement' she found adhesives to be more satisfactory than stitchery.

In this panel she is exploring the illusory quality which shot and satin fabrics have, as well as the direction of light which changes the form of the design completely. Audience participation becomes an important factor in assessing the work, as movement in front and to the side produces different aspects from the same design.

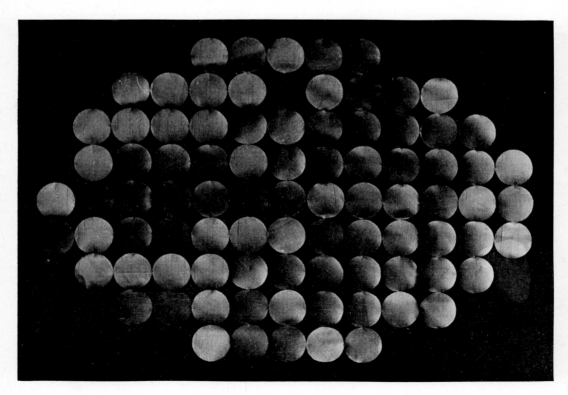

Surge/White Bird/Tiger/by Margaret Kaye   *Collage*

SURGE
WHITE BIRD

The collage works of Margaret Kaye are remarkably fluid whether abstract or figurative in design. Designs are never planned in advance; the artist sometimes has a shape in mind, but for the most part the collage grows from handling the materials.

Rich and sombre colours are used, although in any one work tones are usually very close. Colour and texture control the choice of materials. Background fabrics are frequently wool but a whole range of texture is to be found in applied fabrics. Silk, cotton and wool are included and the jagged scraps of cloth built up in layers, often to a considerable depth.

'Surge' is in strong, rich colours. 'White Bird' is a study in black and white. Both panels dramatically portray atmosphere and movement. 'Tiger' is in soft yellows and greens, all very close in tone, admirably capturing the stealth of the jungle cat.

TIGER

20

Scoobi-Doo/by Olga Moyle

Collage

'Scoobi-doo' is a collage panel inspired by the games French children play with plastic tubing. The whole interest of the work lies in the juxtaposition of unlikely materials, textures and colours. The background is a greenish-gold wild silk upon which are placed squares of hand-woven wool in a brilliant pink. The central shapes are of dull corroded copper surrounded and framed by very fine plastic tubing in fluorescent pinks and orange.

Olga Moyle aims to involve people in the excitement she herself feels in the visual and tactile qualities of materials; to this end she delights in aligning the unlikely: plastic with pure silk, carpet braid with fine cashmere and satin with leather.

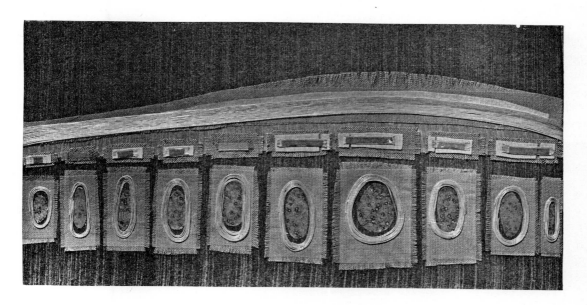

Attic Lion/by Olga Moyle   Collage

This collage was inspired by the
14th century B.C. Lion Gate at
Mycenae. Olga Moyle demonstrates
again her love of unusual materials and
textures, and the aligning of the unlikely.
Textured and patterned materials which
at first glance are very disturbing live
happily together.

The lion, of yellow wild silk, is
decorated and outlined with straw
braid. The background of natural linen
is enriched with pieces of heavily
quilted white cotton. The sun is two
discs of wild silk in streaks of purple
and orange (a manufacturer's reject)
with the rays glittering in gold sequins.
The whole panel is enclosed by a
vibrant and aggressive border of black
and white woollen braiding.

Three Stars/by Christine Risley   Collage and Embroidery

The three stars which form the basis of this work were found by Christine Risley already embroidered on a moth-eaten background. The discovery inspired her to design a surround for them. The motifs were taken from the old ground. With the red outline edge round the stars as a guide, a composition was designed, the whole held together with this kind of line in red and orange tape.

Blocks of squares of felt were added in red and orange, and pink and turquoise. The same colours are repeated in the crosses surrounding the top motif. Quite a lot of gold is used. The shiny squares are gold leather. Gold braid is used in the long lines. The dots are plastic paillettes anchored to the background. The whole presents a clean, uncluttered look of great richness.

Christine Risley is not a haphazard worker. She does not like extraneous matter that does not tie in with her conception of the whole picture. Everything is first designed on squared paper, the design being made the same size as the intended embroidery. Designs are completely worked out before starting. Changes are rarely made. She works rather like an architect, planning and designing until all is quite right, and not until then is the panel started.

Cock and Hen/Angry Gander/Fighting Cocks
by Vera Sherman
Collage

Themes have been drawn from many sources. Bird life, wild and domestic, has been the basis for many collages. Once a subject has been fully investigated and the imagination fired, a recurring theme offers the possibility of endless visual statements. A whole series developed following observations made in a farmyard. Sketches are rarely made and designs are never worked out before starting work. There is however an awareness of the direction or movement a particular piece will take.

Colour being expressive of mood, the colour scheme will have been formulated with the birth of the idea. Strident reds, oranges and yellows are dominant in studies of cockerels. There are softer, quieter tones of orange in the 'Cock and Hen' illustrated here.

Blues and greens are used in the 'Angry Gander'. In this study the stance of the bird rather than the colour expresses the emotive power.

Early textile works were much concerned with embroidery, but in the collages illustrated stitchery is used primarily to give added texture to certain area. The composition generally and the nature of the fabric itself, especially loosely woven cloth which frays easily, are relied upon to convey the mood and movement at which I aim.

FIGHTING COCKS

This Maddening Crowd/Rush Hour/ by Vera Sherman

Collage

Man about his daily business presents endless theme possibilities. The rhythm of the milling crowd upon the city pavements is a source of inspiration to which I return time and time again. To capture that seething mass is a constant challenge whether I am handling clay, paint or fabric. Fabric collage, however, claims more and more of my attention. The tactile qualities of cloth appeal to me as much as the wide variegation of colour.

Colour itself can be a problem. It is often less easy (for me) to find fabric of the exact shade or tone than it would be to mix paint. There is nevertheless ample compensation in the many qualities afforded by fabric, not least the contrasts such as matt and shiny; rough and smooth; thick and thin; transparent and opaque; all bringing a new depth to the same colour.

'Rush Hour' is one of several figure groups based on this theme. 'This Maddening Crowd' was in fact the first of the series, as may be evident, for there is less agitation here than in later works which have followed the development of the idea.

'This Maddening Crowd' is on a mid-green textured linen ground. There is a small orange area, but browns and darkish reds are predominant. The reds have a sheen which adds 'lift' to the area. There is more orange in 'Rush Hour' and the figures cover a greater part of the background, which is grey-green, giving the figures even more dominance and vitality.

Works on ecclesiastical themes are described on pages 95–96.

THIS MADDENING CROWD

Rainbow in the Sky/by Eirian Short   Collage

'Rainbow in the Sky' is from a series by
Eirian Short which has been of
particular interest to young students
who have appreciated the 'Pop Art'
element. The technique is styled
collage, but the artist brings a very
personal approach to the medium. In
this work the clouds are in white
piping cord stuck on to a hardboard
backing. The sky is strips of
hardboard covered with a spun rayon
fabric in several tones of turquoise and
inlaid. Where the rainbow crosses the
clouds, rainbow colours are painted in
Dylon Dyes.

Orange Band/Three Diamonds/Enlargement/ In Blue/Direction/by Anne Butler   Embroidery

Anne Butler's approach to embroidery is very personal. Her concern is with an art form which is purely about embroidery, neither cloth painting nor demonstration of needlepower. She points out that a piece of applied felt may say 'I am flat and composite in construction' as well as saying 'I am a triangular green area'. A woollen thread may say 'I am making knotty red marks' as well as saying 'I am pliable, spiral and soft'.

The simplicity of 'Orange Band' has been arrived at only after careful deliberation. The production of such apparently uncomplicated work is a complex process. Anne Butler's designs are based upon the considerations she feels are relevant to embroidery and she is continually interrelating all these considerations. The background of 'Orange Band' is a black woollen fabric. Applied areas of white felt and orange silk have been turned on to card shapes before being applied. The areas of stitchery are all raised chain bands. Several different types of wool threads have been used and many layers of raised bands cross each other.

'Three Diamonds' is one of a series of panels the compositions of which have become simpler to enable the artist to concentrate on the relationship between weave, texture, surface and scale. The whole surface is about texture, varying in its degree of sophistication and magnification. The background and threads are of wool. The main stitch used is herringbone into which star

ORANGE BAND
THREE DIAMONDS

stitch has been introduced in parts. Straight lines have also been used and french knots in other areas. Two diamonds are knitted and one worked in canvas work—the effect of the three is similar—all are turned on to card and applied.

'Enlargement' has a woollen fabric background with wool thread and appliqué mounted on card and applied. The centre area is worked in herringbone stitch and french knots. The other stitched area is in herringbone only. It is a static design in which movement has been introduced with the direction of the stitchery.

'In Blue' is based upon appliqué fabric turned on to card and applied. Ribbon is also applied. Herringbone and raised chain stitch is worked in wool thread. The background fabric is textured.

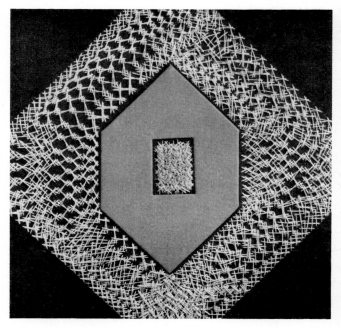

ENLARGEMENT

IN BLUE

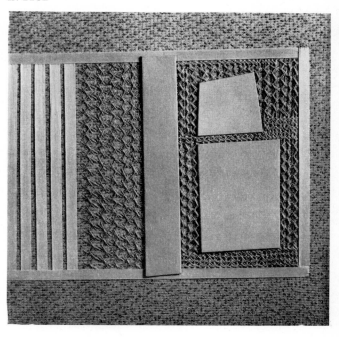

'Direction' is based upon three textural
areas. The background is made up of
two pieces of fabric which join under
the central area. Most of the central
area is worked on a canvas (10 to the
inch) background. The raised areas to
the left have been worked on the
single needle tufting machine, the
balance worked by hand in tent stitch.
The whole piece has been stretched on
to thin hardboard and applied. The light
areas in the lower strip are of fabric
turned on to card and applied.

Another work by Anne Butler is
illustrated on page 98.

Orchid/by Jean Campbell

Embroidery/Gold Work

Jean Campbell's designs are principally derived from natural forms. Shells, rocks, plants and characteristic elements of various types of landscapes and seascapes are the design source of much of her work. 'Orchid' is a representative example. It was developed from analytical drawings of an orchid. A series of collages using a variety of materials followed the initial drawing, resulting in an embroidery using appliqué, padded work, beading, loose couching and gold work. Pieces of celluloid were incorporated with the materials and threads. 'Orchid' is quite small, about 9 inches square, and is one of a series executed by the artist using hand and machine stitchery with added dried plants, shells and pebbles.

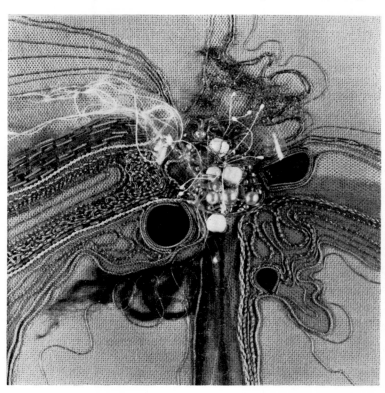

C

Many different hand embroidery stitches have been employed by Jean Carter in 'Wilting Moonflower'. Eyelets, french knots, chain, heavy chain and couching have been executed in threads of varying textures. Matt, shiny, rough and smooth knitting wools and embroidery threads have been used. Beads of wood, plastic sequins and mirror discs have been incorporated. On a cerise coloured background—an Indian hand woven cotton furnishing fabric—the threads are in yellows, reds, oranges, greens and silver.

In this work the artist has expressed her interest in the temporary, short flowering time of certain weeds and garden plants. By the choice of colours and the use of gently curving lines she has conveyed the strong colours and forms coming in quick succession and then wilting away to nothing.

Sunny Summer Flowers/by Jean Carter   Embroidery

Jean Carter's embroideries usually evolve gradually as a result of notes about a word, a theme, a colour or a shape. 'Sunny Summer Flowers' developed from observations made in a garden one sunny day. The variety in arrangement of colour and pattern of small daisy-like flowers has been taken as the theme for the panel.

The artist has used both hand and machine stitchery, observing the disciplines imposed by the selection and use of certain fabrics and threads. Circles are outlined in machine embroidery, details are worked in hand embroidery using couching, french knots, woven webs, eyelets and chain stitches. The background is orange hessian. Shades of orange, pink, red, cerise and purple have been chosen for the linen, cotton and rayon threads and for the knitting, weaving and embroidery wools. Small beads and sequins are also included to show change of texture.

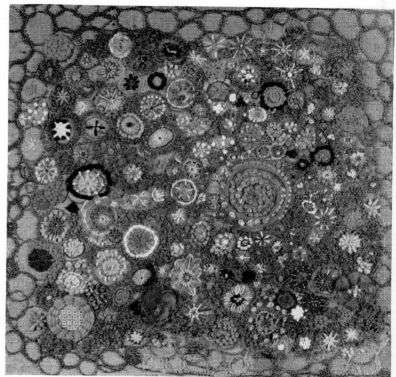

Rock Pools/by Jean Carter

In this panel modern dress fabrics and Victorian dress velvets have been incorporated to good effect. Both hand and machine embroidery have been used.

Taking 'Rock Pools' as her theme, Jean Carter has conveyed the ebb and flow of the water upon rocks. The movement of sand and sea and the changing shapes of the reflected rocks have been suggested by the use of dense and transparent fabrics. These are applied and held in place by machine stitching and couched threads.

On a blue cotton background the dress velvets, pure silks, chiffon, organza and organdie in colours of blue, green, purple, yellow and brown have been applied. Threads in similar colours, wool, mohair, chenille, rayon floss and embroidery cottons together with Victorian bugle beads and modern sequins enrich the whole work.

Magic Flower/by Jean Carter   Embroidery

The idea for 'Magic Flower' was suggested by the sight of dew upon cobwebs, flowers and seedheads. Like most of Jean Carter's embroideries the piece developed as the work progressed. The artist rarely plans in great detail before starting, finding such a method too limiting and dull.

For 'Magic Flower' a background of green textured rayon and cotton furnishing fabric was chosen. The threads are in shades of purple, red, orange, yellow and green; knitting wools, mohair, Lurex, cotton and linen being included. The technique is hand embroidery—couching, criss-cross and straight stitches being employed for the most part. Interest is directed to the effect of colours when changed by the direction of stitches and threads.

Glimpse of Golden Fields/by Jean Carter   *Embroidery*

The theme of 'Glimpse of Golden Fields' is that of landscape. Trees, fields and a stream are contained within a limited area of vision as when viewed through field glasses or a telescope.

On a background of coarse linen the artist has used a wide variety of threads, cotton, wool, linen, rayon and others associated with knotting, weaving and embroidery. Colours include orange, yellow, gold, green, blue, red and purple. Circles in kid and orion cloth are applied. Hand embroidery has been used throughout, the artist exploiting the quality of threads and stitches. The stitches include couching, running, chain and heavy chain, french knots and woven webs.

A panel by Jean Carter on an ecclesiastical theme is illustrated on page 99.

Joy Clucas is well aware that the variety and richness of the materials at the disposal of the embroiderer make it impossible not to be sometimes purely concerned with colour and texture.

'White Development' is for this artist an isolated work; as will be seen elsewhere in this book, she is usually much concerned with machine embroidery. 'White Development' is hand embroidered in shades of white in different types and thicknesses of thread on a linen scrim. Straight stitches have a dramatic impact. The many shades of white have a richness not evident in the illustration.

Warrior/Sun/Metropole/by Rosalind Floyd   Embroidery

The three works, 'Warrior', 'Sun' and 'Metropole', represent two stages in the development of Rosalind Floyd's work. The 'Warrior' and 'Sun' were produced in 1964–66 at a time when her main concern was with aspects of surface. Her approach was immediate and intuitive with very little conscious planning taking place away from the work. 'Metropole' was produced in 1970. Here the surface plays a similar role in the overall effect, but represents one aspect of a more complex and preconceived approach to image building.

In the 'Warrior' and 'Sun' series the artist's interest in surface led her to concentrate on enrichment with consequently less emphasis on colour and complexity of composition. In the case of the 'Warrior' the surface is developed on a simple black silhouette with applied areas of black materials of varying textures, black thread and beads. 'Sun' is on a bright pink ground. The colour is neutralized because the applied threads are restricted to pink and red.

The effect of light upon the surface is also important. The 'Warrior' includes light-reflecting and light-absorbing surfaces. The surface of 'Sun' is developed in depth, making it possible to place rich textures in layers and cast shadows from threads and materials stretched across the space.

In 'Metropole' the surface is dictated by the demands of the composition, not by sensuous interaction. Stitches take on more of the role of linear compositional elements than decorative or textural effects. The whole is a more controlled and austere statement.

SUN

METROPOLE

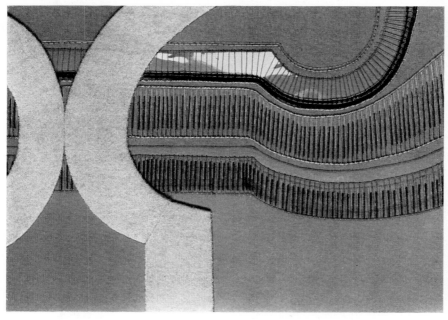

Sun/Nebulae/White Level/Intersection/Summer Field/
Winter Field/by Janet Graham   *Embroidery*

The works illustrated are representative of several stages in the development of Janet Graham's embroidered panels.

'Sun' is from the first stage. It consists mainly of applied fabrics, a few stitches and metal shavings. At this time many of the artist's works were based on circles. Man has always used symbols and geometric shapes in art, but upon reflection Janet Graham thinks she may very well have been

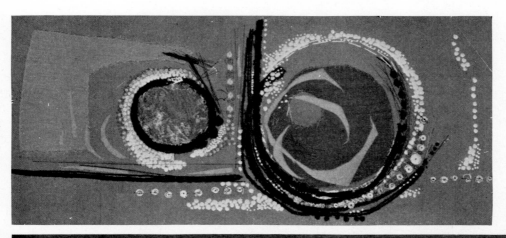

SUN

NEBULAE

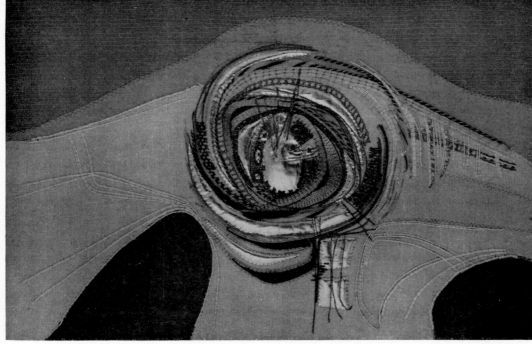

influenced by space exploration and by photographs of the sun and sun-spots. The colours in 'Sun' are suggestive of heat, being variations of orange and red, emphasized by black, which is used to suggest movement.

'Nebulae', worked some time after 'Sun', was influenced by space photography. It uses the complicated and slow technique of gold work. A freedom of design and a feeling of depth is achieved by the star shape in raised gold leather and gold thread (jap gold, bullion, purl and plate) against lemon-yellow and orange velvets and reps. These techniques, fabrics and threads were carefully chosen for richness and sparkle and the subtlety of different shades of gold.

'White Level' and 'Intersection' were worked later than 'Sun' and 'Nebulae'. The design for 'White Level' was influenced by the artist's environment. At the time new roads were being built around Blackheath where she was then living. The panel is worked in various shades of white with ridges of white cotton sheeting sewn on top and raised by means of Italian quilting.

The idea was a simple abstract one, contrasting the rigid thrust of the three oblong shapes with the speckled marks of white wool couched with various coloured threads. The whole achieves a feeling of spontaneity which is not easy with embroidery.

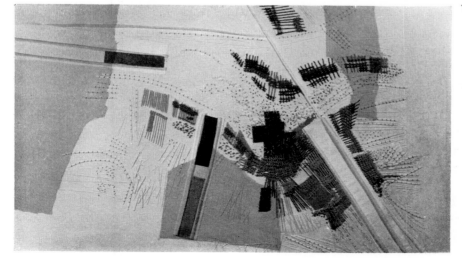

WHITE LEVEL

'Intersection' was the result of observing the flow of traffic from the ninth floor of the College of Fashion in London. The artist's idea was to interpret the movement and the lights and to contrast these with blocks of colour. Much of the embroidery was effected by the choice of threads, Perlita and Sylko perlé which shine rather like artificial light especially on or under organdie and net.

'Summer Field' and 'Winter Field' followed the artist's move from London to Kent. They combine movement and spontaneity with control and balance of design. They are of no particular scene but an accumulated feeling for landscape seen daily. 'Summer Field' records the rhythm and movement of wheat and stubble, the field shapes contrasting with static tree forms. It is worked mainly in running stitch, herringbone and couching in shades of yellow with touches of pinks and blues.

The memory of water movements and sedges against bleak ploughed fields was the beginning of 'Winter Field'. Running stitches in wool are used. Tufting, which subtly changes the thread, making it appear deeper and richer in colour, suggestive of the feathery sedges of the dykes, is also incorporated. The result is a simplification which the artist considers one of her most successful works, coming as it does nearest to her mind-image.

SUMMER FIELD

WINTER FIELD

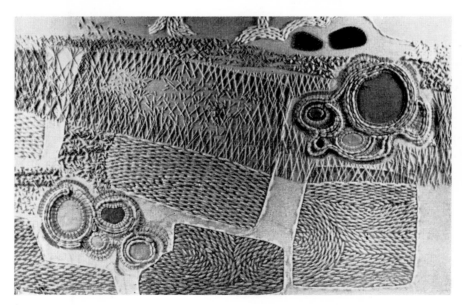

45

'Glass Inset 1' is the first of a series by Cecil O'Donohue incorporating lumpy pieces of annealed glass. A double wool fabric was used and the glass enclosed in 'pockets' between the two surfaces. Areas of the upper surface of the fabric were cut away and pattern darning worked on the exposed lower weave.

To complement the glass colours, different tones of grey/blue and turquoise floss were used for the pattern darning. Bundles of woollen and Fresca threads, in orange and yellow, introduced contrast at intervals over the darned areas.

Gradations of orange and orange-brown Fresca thread and wool, and white gimp, surround the centre group of glass pieces. The heavy two-tone cording, at top and bottom, is couched carpet sisal.

The bars crossing over the glass are part of the upper weave. At the time of working it seemed structurally right to Cecil O'Donohue to reinforce these bars with needleweaving, to help hold the glass in place. Now, when no longer absorbed with the technicalities, she considers the total effect would have been better served by substituting less rigid needlewoven bars over the glass pieces, even if this would have meant sacrificing the use of the cloth structure for this purpose.

Flowing Trees/by Heather Padfield   Embroidery

Heather Padfield has taken landscape
themes for the basis of many of her
embroidered panels. The composition
of 'Flowing Trees' features a
section of landscape viewed from the
opposite slope of a heavily wooded
valley in Wales. The panel dramatizes
a visual dialogue between the smooth,
glass-like serenity of the field and the
mysteriously changing colours and
contours of foreground trees. The
reflective quality of gold kid and cord,
gold passing, Lurex, sequins and silk
threads creates an impression of a
low-angled evening sun.

'The Downs' by Heather Padfield
consists of a series of visual analogies
representing the unique characteristics
of chalk structured landscape. In
particular the crisp dry tones and
textures of spring cultivated fields are
emphasized by the use of natural
coloured hessian and open-weave
white furnishing fabrics.

The granular textures and closely
defined light and shade produced by
this type of geological formation are
symbolized by textured raffia, wool and
Perlita thread. The composition is
dominated by strong rhythmic pattern
created by furrows and perimeters
pushing up from the left of the
composition.

Golden Meadow by Anne Maile (see page 79)

Cross and Crown of Thorns by Janet Warner (see page 101)

Sun/by Heather Padfield   Embroidery

'Give me the splendid silent sun with
all his beams full-dazzling.'
                              —Walt Whitman.

This embroidery by Heather Padfield
is a conceptional symbolism using
suede and leather appliqué. A feeling of
radiating light is obtained with linear
silk and gold embroidery. The
background is a textured woollen cloth
with a fleck of orange in the weave.
The dark strip to the right is a panel of
deep violet silk.

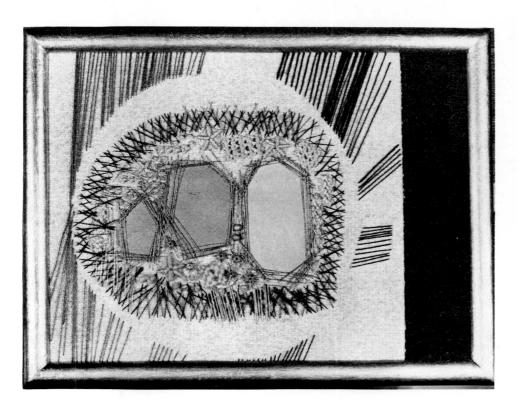

D

Black has been used throughout in
'Black Beauty' by Eirian Short, and an
arresting panel produced by the careful
selection and application of texture and
pattern. The background has been
patterned on the Cornely stitch
machine. Shapes in 'mock croc' PVC,
and velvet have been applied, and
beads in varying sizes, a mixture of
wood, glass jet and plastic, added.
The body shape has been padded with
Terylene wadding.

Evening Sun/by Eirian Short

A traditional embroidery pattern has been used by Eirian Short as a basis for 'Evening Sun'. The lower half of the large 5 feet 6 inches by 3 feet panel is in Florentine pattern. Worked on rug canvas, strips of fabric have been used instead of the customary wool.

The sun shape is applied, a woven rayon satin in a checked pattern being used. The halo around the sun has been made by pushing roughly torn strips of transparent fabric, organdie, chiffon and net through from the back. Pastel colours are used throughout.

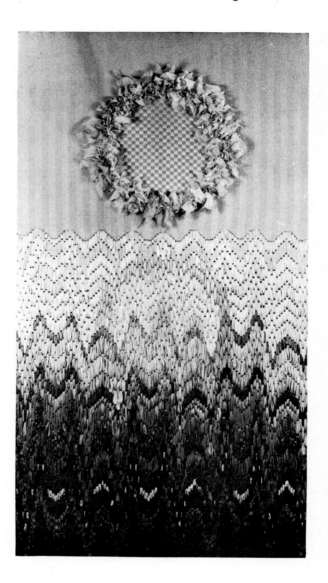

Nasturtium/by Audrey Tucker   Embroidery

Before embarking upon 'Nasturtium'
Audrey Tucker carried out several
exploratory drawings of a nasturtium
head as a basis for the growth of a
design idea. These were made in oil,
pastels and a variety of pencils from
B to 6B. The drawings brought out the
raised linear pleated type texture of the
flower, giving lines of colour change
moving around the background petal
areas. A series of drawings were then
carried out breaking down the original
into a pattern of large shapes with lines
of colour.

Although now an abstract shape, it was
important to keep the original quality
of texture in the embroidery. Shapes of
colour were applied in dyed muslin
and stitched in blocks of widely spaced
long and short stitch. A raised technique
was used for the lines of colour.
Threads wound around pieces of cane
in colour blocks were arranged and
applied to the background. A final
couched line was added to give a
feeling of broken crusty shapes linking
the embroidered areas into a flower
form.

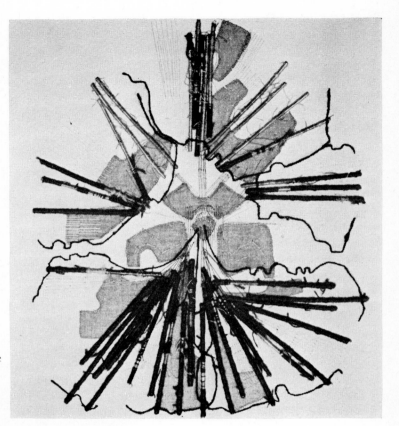

Tranquil Yellow/by Janet Warner　　　　*Embroidery*

A study of seed pods resulted in a series
of embroideries by Janet Warner.
'Tranquil Yellow' is from this series.
The design is bold, with flowing
shapes and clear colours. The colours
are yellows, lime and orange on a
yellow background.

The work is as much collage as
stitchery. The designer is concerned
with the contrasting qualities of flat
applied areas and surface stitchery. She
uses many types of thread to achieve
contrasts. In 'Tranquil Yellow'
precisely placed stitches, mostly french
knots and couching, follow the lines of
the felt shapes applied to the rougher
textured ground.

Another work by Janet Warner is
illustrated in full colour opposite
page 49 and described on page 101.

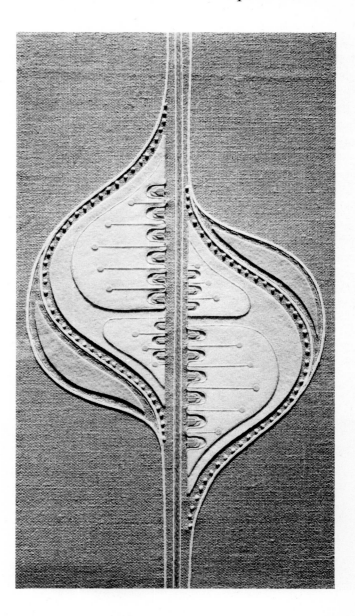

Fireworks/by Joy Clucas

Machine Embroidery

This is an early work by Joy Clucas
from the first 'Contemporary
Hangings' exhibition. It is markedly
decorative in conception. Since that
time the designer has worked
progressively towards pure abstraction
in her embroidered panels.

In 'Fireworks' the bulk of the work is
carried out in machine applied
Twilley's Bubbly knitting yarn on
dark grey cotton rep in white, cream
and pink. The centres are hand-
embroidered in oranges, reds and
pinks. The background is textured with
machine stitching in shades of rich deep
blues and greens.

Fantasy/by Joy Clucas

The idea for 'Fantasy' was formulated when considering a centrepiece for an important exhibition to be held at the Embroiderers' Guild. The work measures 9 feet by 3 feet 6 inches and hangs freely from a metal batten.

The background is black sail-cloth. The motifs are worked in machine stitching and machine applied threads. The threads are comprised of many shades of white, beige, grey-green and grey-brown, with touches of burnt orange.

Winter/by Joy Clucas

'Winter' by Joy Clucas aims to show the stark quality of the season by means of contrast and simplicity. The simple semi-circle of the red half sun contrasts with the long flowing white lines of the central area and the dark green foreground. Contrast is also provided by the textural snow and ice area and the plain but rich fabrics above and below it. The background of the panel is white organdie; the hardboard beneath is sprayed with black, purple and red paint, giving a delicate colour change to the sky. The embroidery consists of a variety of white threads applied with machine.

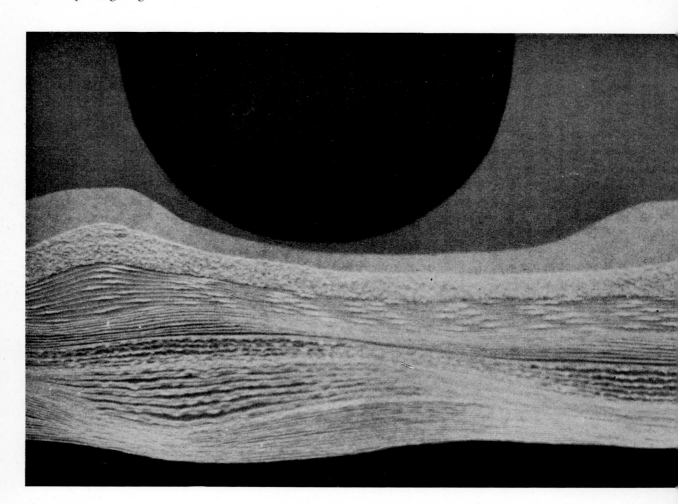

Joy Clucas has frequently taken the elements as a theme for her embroidered panels. 'Cyclone' is worked with plain and textured knitting yarns applied by machine, the outer shapes being fine machine drawing. The colours are basically greens and blues on a blue ground. There is movement in the revolving shapes; there is also a restfulness in the cool colouring and the simplicity of the shapes dovetailing together.

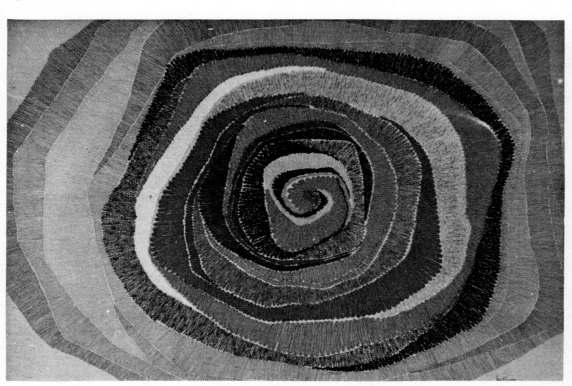

Dawn/by Joy Clucas

Machine Embroidery

The abstraction of landscape for painter and embroiderer alike is an absorbing theme. In 'Dawn' Joy Clucas portrays buildings shrouded in mist. The background material is red, the white Vilene shapes are overlaid with shades of pale blue net. Purple and black net are worked lightly into the sky and more heavily into the foreground. The sky and the mist areas are in pink, orange and pale blues.
The whole work gives an atmosphere of stillness and peace.

Solar Night/by Joy Clucas   Machine Embroidery

Apart from the romantic aspect of suns and moons a sense of restfulness and tranquillity purely sensual is experienced when gazing at a circle. It is a symbol of completeness and continuity.

The inspiration to be found in themes of space is endless. 'Solar Night' is in this vein and the culminating panel of a series by Joy Clucas. The background of the work is turquoise green rayon. The small sun shape on the left is cream rayon, the large one purple rayon. The sun shape on the right has been produced by several layers of orange net. Fine green and blue nets give soft colour changes to the sky area and pink and brown to the earth area. The whole is built up with machine stitching, some of which is in shaded thread and some invisible thread. The latter gives a soft glint to the sun shapes.

Form Emerging/by Joy Clucas   Machine Embroidery

This work appears in full colour opposite page 64.

Artists, poets and musicians have been concerned with the wonders of the Creation from time immemorial. It is inevitable that this should have been used as a source of inspiration as many times in embroidery as in other art forms. Joy Clucas has worked many machine embroidered panels on this theme. 'Form Emerging' is from this series.

The artist intended that the work should convey the majesty and the awe of the subject. The surface has the richness and decorative quality indicative of the use of applied threads. The threads are in brilliant oranges, pinks and purples on an orange dupion ground. This is a representation of the cooling of burning gases and the form of the world emerging. There is no texture on the background, this would have detracted from the feeling of form emerging from emptiness. Even though the colours merge, the applied wools are in strong textural contrast with the smooth background.

Gold Block/by Joy Clucas   ## Machine Embroidery

This panel demonstrates an unusual approach to method and material. For 'Gold Block' Joy Clucas has utilized the soft pliable threads of a cotton vegetable bag as the background for machine embroidery. The threads distort slightly during working, giving an interest to the lines and shapes.

Small pieces of gold and yellow fabric show through the open parts. The simple shapes are enriched by subtle colour changes.

A hand embroidered panel by Joy Clucas is illustrated on page 39.

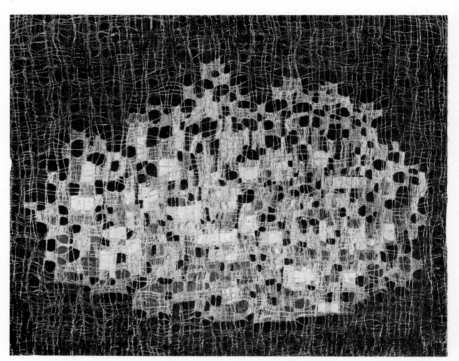

DETAIL OF ABOVE

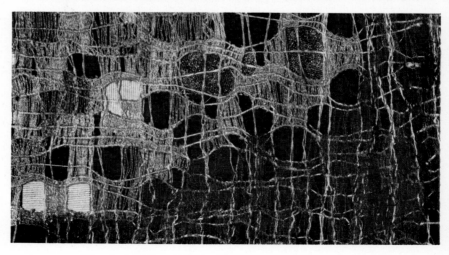

Church Steeple/by Cynthia Pearson   Machine Embroidery

Ideas arising from a study of
architectural forms resulted in a series
of machine embroidered panels by
Cynthia Pearson. She has made a study
of church buildings, often concentrating
on a single aspect—a porch, a tower or
windows. The inspiration for 'Church
Steeple' came from a view of the
steeple seen from below and through
trees.

The background fabric is patterned in
broad stripes in tones of pink. Red
woollen yarn, previously crimped,
provides the rough textured area.
The texture on the steeple has been
achieved by stitching down a variety of
silks and crêpes with the automatic
embroidery patterns on a domestic
sewing machine. The surface of the
foliage has been created by chiffons,
thick woollen yarn and stitchery.

Mexican Sun/by Eirian Short

Macramé is a very ancient form of decorative knotting which originated in the Middle East and spread from there through the world. Normally it was worked in geometric designs for braids, fringes and the like. Eirian Short has used the basic macramé knots, the flat knot and the half-hitch, in a completely free way. The main threads—a mixture of wool, cotton, chenille, string, silk, rayon and raffia—were set on to a curtain ring in the centre and knotted outwards. New threads were added when colour changes were required during the progress of work. Hot colours predominate—reds, pinks and oranges. The light area is yellow. The sun shape was drawn on to a board and the knotting done over this. Beads were slipped on where required. Upon completion the work was mounted on to a plain woven fabric of kingfisher blue.

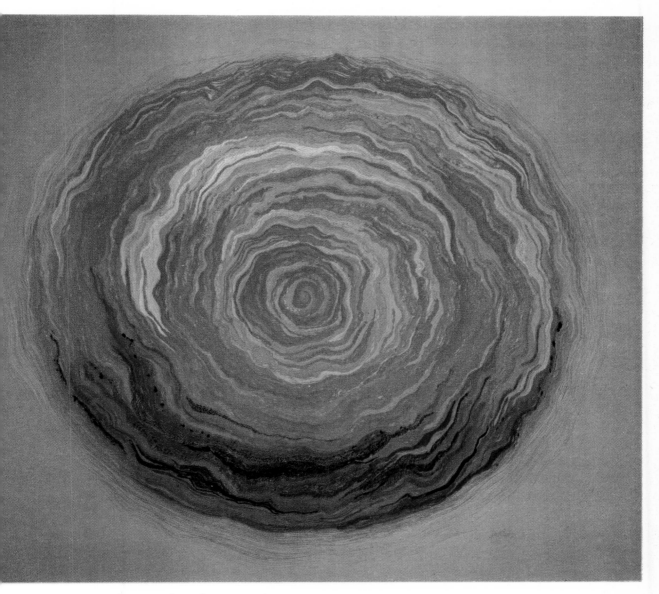

Form Emerging by Joy Clucas (see page 61)

Poise by Anne Maile (see page 79)

Year In—Year Out/by Eirian Short   *Macramé*

Eirian Short has taken the changing seasons as the theme for many of her works. Frequently the technique is based upon traditional stitchery interpreted in a highly contemporary manner.

'Year In—Year Out', a hanging approximately 3 feet square, has been worked in macramé. Mixed threads have been used including wool, raffia and dyed chenille. Dyed wooden beads are incorporated, complementing the softer shapes created by the flat knot balls. Cording over a wooden ring is used for the sun symbol. The changing colours, dark blues, through greens, yellows, red to red-brown, symbolize the seasons.

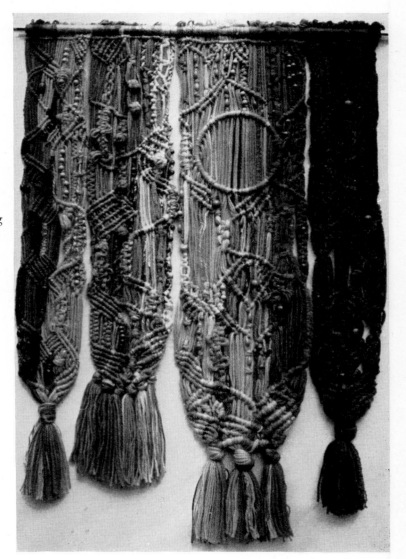

Rings and Things/by Eirian Short

'Rings and Things' is another macramé work by Eirian Short, a detail of which is illustrated here. It is a slender hanging some 4 feet long, worked mainly in cording over metal rings of varying sizes. Knitting wools in the primary colours—red, blue and yellow—have been used.

Works created by Eirian Short in other techniques are illustrated on pages 10, 29, 50–51 and 97.

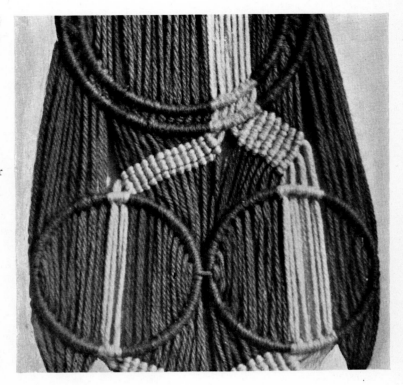

Winter/Sun over the Waves/by Tadek Beutlich   Tapestry

'Winter' by Tadek Beutlich is woven
in the traditional technique of tapestry
weaving. In stark black, white and
grey, it is a striking design symbolizing
the wintry scene. The weft is woollen
yarn of the same thickness throughout,
giving a characteristic flat surface to the
work.

WINTER

A mixture of tapestry and plain weave
has been combined in 'Sun over the
Waves'. Spun and unspun wool has
been used in the weft as well as other
materials including unspun jute and
hemp. Some parts of the weft have
been omitted, showing the warp only.
The different thicknesses and textures
give the work a three-dimensional
effect.

Other hangings by Tadek Beutlich are
illustrated on pages 80–81 and 102.

SUN OVER THE WAVES

DETAIL OF ABOVE

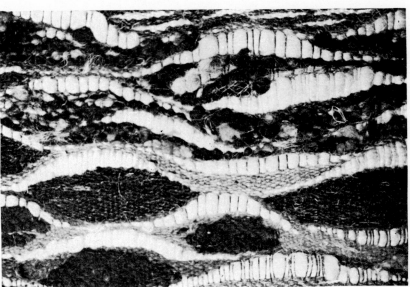

Abstract VIII/*Trio*/*Fossil Strata*/*by Eleanor Scarfe   Tapestry*

Eleanor Scarfe has developed a very
personal weaving technique. Her
panels are two-dimensional solid
weavings using mostly wool, but
sometimes incorporating beads,
metallic threads and tweedy mixtures.
Texture is achieved as well as shape
and colour.

The advantage of her technique is that
the apparatus is very simple and
portable. There is no hard and fast
commitment to an original design
because each line is not completed at a
time as on a traditional loom. Shapes
can be shifted along the warp; straight
lines become curves, solid areas
perforated and these perforations filled.

'Abstract VIII' is an experiment in
colour illusion. The outer edge of the
red 'eye' in the centre of the black
shape gives the illusion that there is a
purple rim around it. The background
has been given texture by weaving
different lengths of a fine black wool
together with coarse white thread. This
has resulted in a pattern that is
irregular.

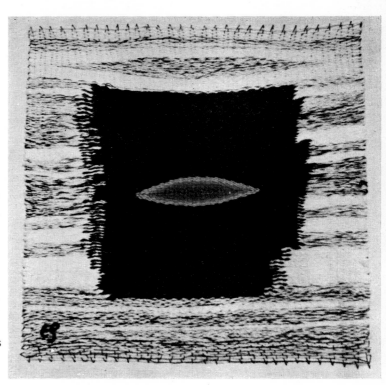

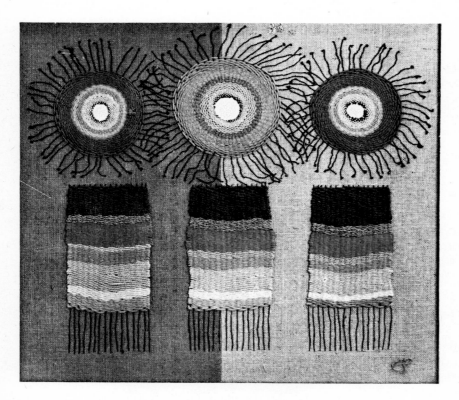

'Trio' is one of a series that started as
an idea stimulus for students. It
shows that a simple card loom can
become the means of creating endless
colour relationships. The circles are
concentric rings of colour, they relate
to each other and also to their
background. In this example, the
colours of the circles are brilliant and
almost primary. The background is of
bright red and bright yellow hessian.

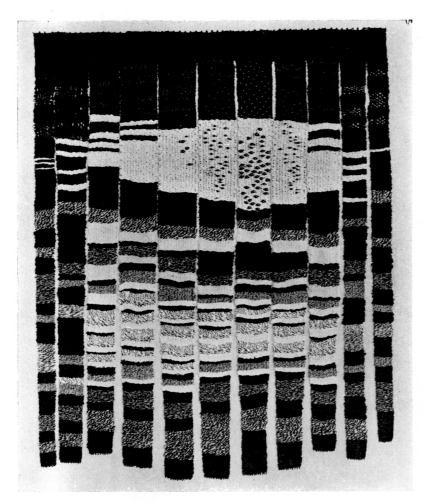

There are two variations of the striking black and white tapestry 'Fossil Strata'. These large panels, woven as separate 'ties', were designed as possible 'room dividers'. With heavy weights at the ends they should have hung rather like bead curtains. In practice, they were not rigid enough and so were applied to stretched linen backgrounds to make decorative panels. With the 'Fossil Strata' series Eleanor Scarfe started to incorporate beads into her tapestries. It is a series in which she deliberately uses a wide range of natural and synthetic threads and plastics.

Details of a hanging by Eleanor Scarfe based on an ecclesiastical theme are to be found on page 103.

Forest/Wart Hog/In Full Bloom/Special Bloom/Asteroid/
Industry/Imagination/Around and About/Golden Meadow/
Poise/Giraffes/by Anne Maile   Tie and Dye

Anne Maile has diligently researched
the ancient craft of tie and dye,
experimented extensively with modern
dyes and in the process created many
new methods.

Tie and dye designs are produced by
manipulating, binding and sewing the
fabric so that during the dyeing process
some parts resist the dye. The effect is
'organic' in design in that it is made
by the dye spreading and growing. It is
another type of resist dyeing (see batik
pages 11–15).

Anne Maile's technical expertise
coupled with an innate feeling for
nature and a knowledge of botany are
markedly demonstrated in all her work.
Her design sources are manifold. They
can, however, be roughly divided into
two, those which exploit different
techniques to produce a united whole
and those which utilize the effect of the
technique to express a visual image.

Three main methods are used by the
artist to approach the craft; rarely is
any one method confined to any one

FOREST

work. The first is to draw and stitch the design directly on the cloth. Then to pull the threads up tightly and form the cloth into a bundle of closely packed gathers.

This method of drawing and sewing was used for 'Forest'. The design exploits the lacy 'resist' produced by the sewing method to interpret the structure of trees. Fine oversewing depicts the small branches and distant trees, contrasting with the coarser stitches for trunks and foreground.

The same method was used for 'Wart Hog', 'In Full Bloom' and 'Special Bloom'. 'Wart Hog' is in deep yellow/orange, the material being fine cotton. The background was created by the technique characteristically known as marbling. In 'In Full Bloom' the flower areas were sewn, dyed red and then bunched up with loose stitches to reserve the colour. The whole panel was again dyed in various shades of green. The result is a composition suggestive of serenity and harmony. 'Special Bloom' is in colours

WART HOG

of pumpkin, orange, crimson and maroon. It is on thick silk. Attention has been centred on one flower head. The eye is drawn to the heart of the flower by the scintillating blue of the inner petals.

IN FULL BLOOM

ASTEROID

The second method of approach is to tie objects in the cloth. 'Asteroid', on a cotton fabric, was produced this way. The star-like shape is composed of radials of alternating width. These were created by tying small and medium sized stones in the cloth along previously drawn lines. Dominant colours are yellow, orange and brown.

The third method relies on the folding, pleating or rolling of the material before binding and dyeing. This was used for 'Industry', 'Around and About' and 'Imagination'. 'Industry' gives the feeling of power radiating from a central force. It is full of pulsating vitality, symbolic of industrial life. 'Around and About' is an apt title for the work, a square of silk tie-dyed to produce a circumrotatory composition in blues, rich purple and crimson. 'Imagination' is of silk, the vivid scarlet background representative of the mind alive with ideas which radiate and spread out from it in fine vein-like traceries.

INDUSTRY

IMAGINATION
AROUND AND ABOUT

A further development of Anne Maile's work has been a series of tie and dye collages and embroidered appliqués. 'Golden Meadow' (reproduced in full colour opposite page 48) was built up from small pieces of variously patterned tie-dyed cloth. The motifs were cut out, assembled and affixed by adhesive to a tie-dyed background. For 'Poise' (in full colour opposite page 65) the background cloth of cotton was dyed orange and red. Using a fabric of silk and cotton mixture the separate flower motif was tie-dyed in pink, mauve and maroon. The flower shape was then cut out and rearranged. Tiny invisible stitches secure the cut pieces to the background.

Simple tie and dye methods were used to pattern the cotton cambric and flannelette for 'Giraffes'. This work appears in full colour opposite page 80. The shapes of the animals were cut out and pasted on to other tie-dyed fabrics assembled to suggest a landscape. This work was designed to demonstrate to young children the uses to which scraps of tie-dyed cloth can be put and assembled in picture form.

With the visual images in mind, Tadek Beutlich works on several projects at the same time, never using elaborate preparations. He has a fluid approach to materials, techniques and surfaces.

Thick unspun jute and sisal are looped and tufted; different thicknesses of yarn incorporated, resulting in a three-dimensional surface no longer flat as in traditional tapestry. (See pages 67–71.) X-ray film, charred wood veneers and honesty seeds are woven into a warp of loosely woven thin linen—spaced 8 ends per inch—as in 'Wallhanging', a work which also has camelhair and horsehair in the weft.

The detail from 'Talisman', which appears on page 81 after the colour plates, illustrates the warp of black mohair and weft of wool and unspun jute which was dyed by the artist. Plain weave has been combined with leno-weave.

WALLHANGING

Giraffes by Anne Maile (see page 79)

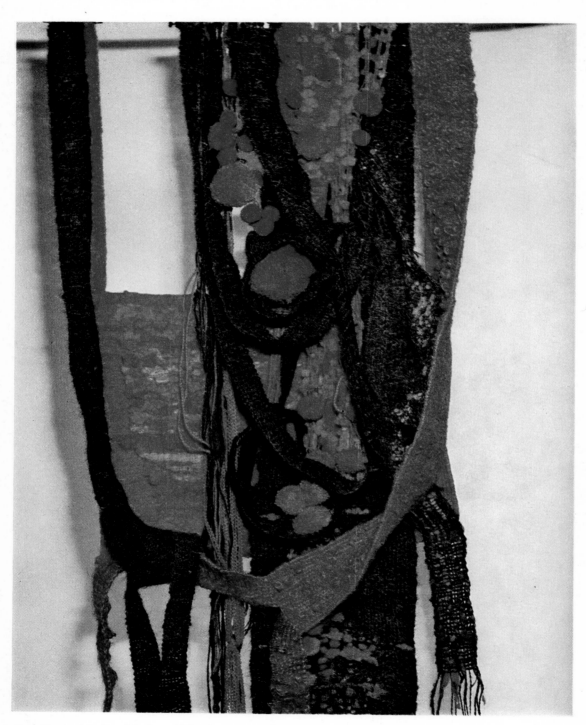

Red Composition by Myriam Gilby (see page 87)

TALISMAN BY
TADEK BEUTLICH

Corduroy Rug/by Peter Collingwood

The traditional method of making a pile rug is the very slow and uneconomical one of tying tufts of wool to the warp. A much quicker method, first used by Alastair Morton around 1950, is corduroy, in which loops are woven automatically and later cut to make the pile. Peter Collingwood developed this method to give a closer pile and has produced many striking designs. 'Corduroy Rug', illustrated here, is in black and white. It is 3 feet by 5 feet and has a wool pile and linen warp.

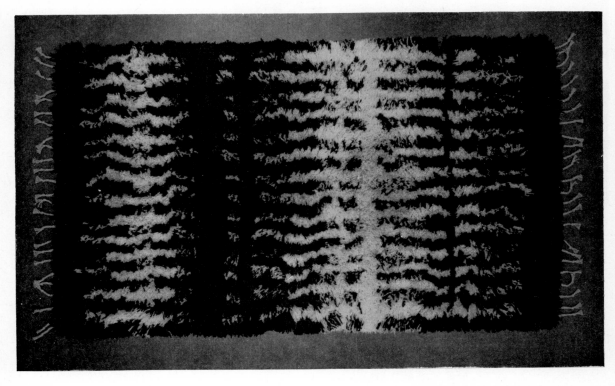

Macrogauze/by Peter Collingwood

By altering the basic parts of a loom
Peter Collingwood found a method of
crossing strips of warp over each other.
This technique, which he called
macrogauze, is simple, quick and
suitable for wall hangings. The
discovery led to many designs
impossible to weave on a conventional
loom. The design illustrated is made of
black and white linen with thin
wooden dowels and measures 31 inches
by 84 inches.

'Abacus' is the outcome of three trains of thought and exploration. Win Evans had woven several hangings which used warp-faced spaced warps with the capability of holding wood or metal rods which she finds has sympathy of texture and quality with either wool or heavy linen threads.

In 'Abacus' the spaced warps were developed further by their individual treatment, the separate warps being divided further into three woven or unwoven sections. The second development was the introduction of pattern in the warps with a loom woven simulation of tablet weaving. This enabled her to produce circular patterns in the warps which echoed the shapes of the wooden balls appearing between the warps. These balls are threaded on to brazing rods which act as periodic wefts.

The third line of thought involved the use of mathematical sequences, applied to a number of design units. This type of design retains a perennial interest to the observing eye, the result being sufficiently subtle in its all-over effect to allow the observer to seek and find varied pattern sequences.

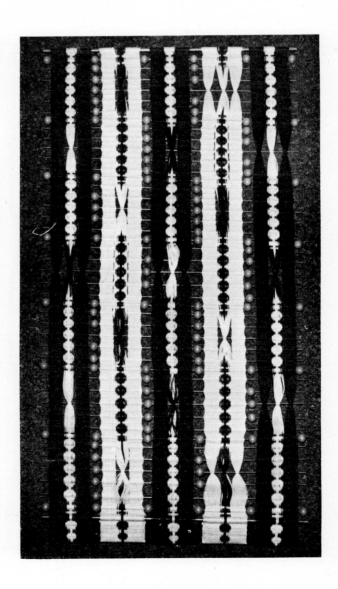

Myriam Gilby was born and lived for many years in India. The memory of colours and shapes encountered there has had a lasting effect upon her work. In the Salem District the local weavers set up their warps on the roadside. The startling colour combinations under the twisting aerial roots of the banyan trees have provided much of the inspiration for both painting and weaving.

The idea for 'Contrasts' was found however at the Lullingstone Silk Farm. It arose from the opposition of surfaces and tensions observed in the hanks of raw silk waste hanging to dry against a white wall. The idea originated from the visual experience, but the layout of the hanging was based on material found in the work area.

The hanging is in black and white, but many subtleties are obtained from the interplay of warm light-absorbing whites of the cottons to the cold light-reflecting silks. Similarly the harshness and vibrancy of horsehair offers a foil to the soft brown-black of the unspun wool. Great variety is also offered in the fabric itself—freely hanging warps in opposition to the tensions of the formally woven tapestry.

White Composition/by Myriam Gilby   *Weaving*

The hangings of Myriam Gilby reveal
evidence of her early training as a
sculptor, being more low-reliefs which
happen to be in textile rather than
formal tapestries. The artist does not
work to a preconceived plan; her
ideas come as a chain reaction to
solving problems as the work proceeds.
Her ideas grow from a texture, colour
or material which has excited her.

'White Composition' has a cotton and
rayon warp. The weft contains loops of
jute and sisal, giving an additional
three-dimensional effect. It was woven
on a simple weaving frame based on a
free adaptation of those used by the
Navajo Indians.

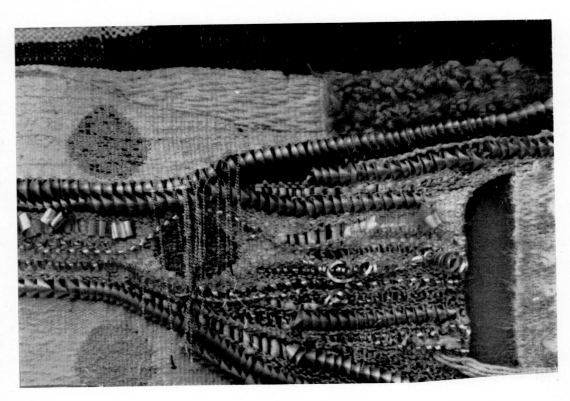

Red Composition/by Myriam Gilby   *Weaving*

This work appears in full colour opposite page 81.

'Red Composition' by Myriam Gilby was woven on a simple rug frame using two warps. The base is of old wool with a semi-circle of dyed unspun wool. Hanging warps are of horsehair and sisal with various gimps, many being bound and twisted together as in Mexican and Peruvian work. A further feature is the bound warps over horsehair and unspun wool loops.

Myriam Gilby developed the design freely, having first prepared a very rough sketch outlining the main rhythmic lines and structural masses.

Weaving techniques pose their own problems and dictate solutions which in turn alter the design. The interest and compulsion to evaluate solutions enables the artist to sustain a vitality of approach throughout the long weaving process.

The red balls in 'Red Composition' resulted from a friend tying coloured balls to the uncompleted warp as a joke at Christmastime. The accent and rhythmic effect of the three-dimensional shapes playing against the linear nature of the free-hanging warps was exactly what the designer needed. A slight alteration in the design concept resulted, using the balls as points of rest, or accents, in an ascending or descending rhythm.

Many of the techniques Myriam Gilby uses are taken directly from primitive manipulatory techniques. Some are used without any need to adapt them to a modern concept, others serve as the basis for a new idea. One of her pleasures in weaving is in discovering the relevance of techniques from the ancient past and in enjoying their use in her own work.

Black Hole/by David Holbourne   Weaving

Having discovered the usefulness of
rope David Holbourne became so
intrigued with its qualities that he now
uses rope or coarse sisal twine almost
exclusively to make space dividers and
sculptural toys, as well as hangings and
sculptures.

'Black Hole' is one of several hangings
that half hang on the wall and half rest
on the floor. Most of these are flat
weavings with three-dimensional rope
coils hanging from them. The coils
rest on the floor.

A young friend of the artist arranged
one of these hangings in the form of an
octopus with the ropes radiating out
from the weaving. This gave David
Holbourne the idea of a structure with
the 'fringe' going upwards. To
emphasize this reversal he made the
weaving three-dimensional so that it
stood out from the wall and occupied
the floor space in front of the hanging.
The rope coils were arranged as flat
to the wall as possible.

The artist's small daughter is fascinated
with the scraps from her father's
workshop. She makes patterns with
them. This plus the incident of the
octopus led David Holbourne to make
what he calls 'change-it' sculptures.
These are basic sculptures with several
movable rope parts. They are a direct
development of the hangings. They are
colourful and whether used as play or
decorative objects are works of art in
their own right with an appeal for
children and adults alike.

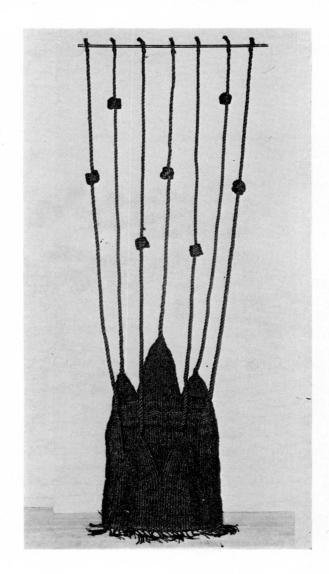

Hanging with Coil/by David Holbourne   *Weaving*

'Hanging with Coil' by David Holbourne is sculptural in concept even though it is mainly flat weaving. Woven in wool with the coiled rope of sisal, the chevrons are in yellow, orange and black. To the designer the shape on the wall is more important than the colour areas within it. He uses them only to accentuate the form.

The hanging was woven soon after David Holbourne began making sculptures of coiled or knotted rope, and he wanted to introduce some of these new forms into his hangings. In this work the rope ends are tied into the fabric. An alternative he has used is to untwist the rope end and use the separated strands as a warp. Hanging these three-dimensional forms back on the wall led to other three-dimensional hangings of lighter, more flexible material which no longer needed to be self-supporting.

Hanging in Grey Linen/by David Holbourne   Weaving

Texture is the basis of all weaving and 'Hanging in Grey Linen' is a small weaving by David Holbourne emphasizing this quality. A more or less high relief composition is the outcome.

'Hanging in Grey Linen' is made entirely of a moderately shiny grey linen to stress the form of the weaving rather than the texture of the yarn. The techniques used are soumak (a rug technique producing a zigzag effect), crochet chains caught up in the weaving and braids tied into the weaving.

David Holbourne's ideas come mainly from trying to extend the possible uses of a particular material, the opposite approach to the artist who uses anything he can lay his hands on to achieve the required effect. He never prepares a finished design before starting work. He finds that answers to problems, and new ideas, suggest themselves more readily when work is in progress than when confronted with an unco-operative piece of paper.

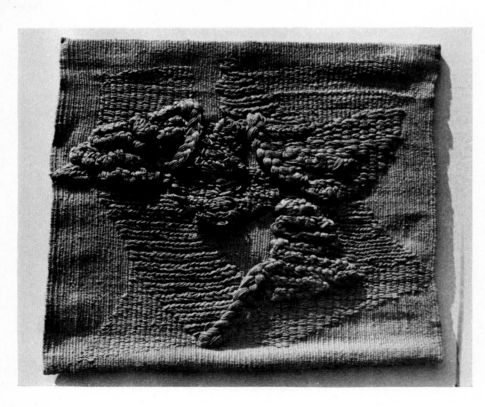

The illustration centres on a detail of a large double-weave hanging by Ruth Hurle. This is one of a pair of inlay and gauze hangings by the artist conceived as part of a general decorative scheme featuring a fine Chinese scroll painting. The threads are therefore in their natural-colour state. Warp and weft are of mixed linen and hand-spun tussore silk. Different thicknesses of thread are used.

The artist considers that weaving plays an important part as a support emphasizing another art form, as in 'Abstract Tree'; as a craft allied to a need; and above all standing in its own right as a method of self-expression.

Seadrift/by Barbara Sawyer

Weaving

Barbara Sawyer is interested in the different textures of natural and synthetic fibres; she collects materials such as wood, perspex and cane and these are often woven into her hangings. Driftwood is picked up from the seashore; the pounding of the seas having smoothed and rounded the edges, the wood is particularly suitable for weaving.

'Seadrift' contains such driftwood. The wood creates small 'checks' in the weave. Warp and weft are of linen, natural and dyed.

Part 2—Ecclesiastical

Resurrection II/by Richard Box   *Collage*

This is one of several variations by Richard Box which shows God the Father receiving the Son. Here he treats the drapery as a flame-like shape denoting the Holy Spirit encompassing both Father and Son, thus making the One Trinity.

'Resurrection II' is carried out in greens and blues to convey peace and rest. Beads and jewels are worked in to help represent joy, hope, glory and the forgiveness of sins. In the simplest way the artist has transcribed visually the doctrinal meaning of the Resurrection.

Another collage by Richard Box is illustrated on page 17.

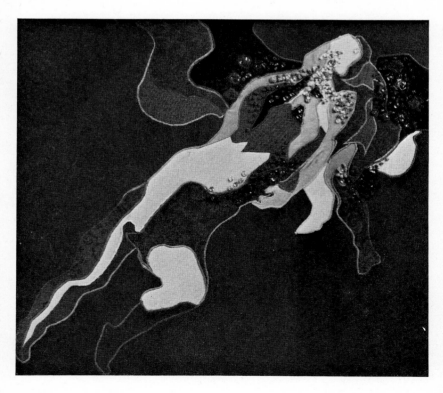

On the Mount/King and Martyr/Saint George by Vera Sherman

Collage

Studies made for secular themes became a natural basis for ecclesiastical panels. The cockerel and its association with St. Peter are obvious, several works were produced based on St. Peter's denial. The bird was treated symbolically, the aim being to convey both defiance and remorse.

'On the Mount' followed an earlier collage based upon scenes witnessed at Speakers Corner in London's Hyde Park. I was anxious to portray the magnitude of the crowd without detracting from the central figure, and to include figures of children, so often absent from classical treatments of the theme. On a blue-grey background the rising ground has been suggested by net. Small stitches were used to attach the net; adhesive, which I use a great deal, being unsuitable for transparent fabrics. The central figure is of brownish grey matt material. Texture and colour are concentrated on the figures in the crowd.

The theme of 'King and Martyr' (in full colour overleaf) came to mind when arranging an exhibition for the Church of St. Edmund King and Martyr. First thoughts were for a 'thrust' of staves from the right-hand foreground towards the martyred figure on the left. In fact as the work progressed the figure was moved towards the centre. At one time it was silhouetted as upon a crucifix and a little of that feeling remains. A growing number of figures pressed forward, subsequently covering many of the staves.

ON THE MOUNT

95

Initially the colour scheme was to be unquestionably red and gold. This was amended when I found the dark blue velvet and the knobbly black tweed flecked with white, blue, red and green. The textural and tonal contrasts it afforded and the 'atmosphere' its inclusion created are valuable to the composition. Whilst working I was unaware of the 'stained glass' effect which has since been commented upon by others.

'Saint George', which appears overleaf in full colour, followed an exhibition arranged for a church dedicated to the saint. Here I wanted to express the triumph of Good over Evil. The universality of the heroic theme was obviously transmitted, because when the hanging was exhibited in America the public associated it with Don Quixote and the work was ultimately re-titled 'Eroica'.

The red fabric is patterned with gold which catches and reflects the light. The retreating figures are in darker reds, blues and mauves; smooth and textured materials are incorporated.

King and Martyr by Vera Sherman (see page 95)

Saint George by Vera Sherman (see page 96)

Creation/by Eirian Short   *Collage*

The illustration shows a detail from 'Creation' by Eirian Short—a panel 6 feet square. Technically the method of working is based upon traditional patchwork, here executed in a very contemporary manner. The entire design was first transferred in line on to hardboard, then cut up with an electric fretsaw. Each piece was then covered with the appropriate fabric and the whole re-assembled as a jigsaw, without stitchery. A background of hardboard was used. Simple symbols were employed for the sun, moon, stars, water and growing things. The tones are carefully graded from dark to light across the design to symbolize the coming of light.

Details of other works by Eirian Short can be found on pages 10, 29, 50–51 and 64–66.

In the embroidered panel 'Symbols'
Anne Butler uses the symbolism of the
circle for Eternity, the cross form and
three nails for the Crucifixion.

On an orange linen ground, the circles
in sharp lemons and green are composed of felt shapes, some of which
are padded. The couched threads are of
woven slub wool.

Let everything that hath breath praise the Lord/
by Jean Carter

Embroidery

The Creation was in the thoughts of Jean Carter when contemplating 'Let everything that hath breath praise the Lord'. She considered the cycle of Creation, life and death, night and day, the seasons of the year, plants, sea creatures and insects, and the need of one for the other and their similarity one to another. She was concerned also with contrasts—the contrast of hot and cold colours and textures rough and smooth, matt and shiny.

Felt has been applied to even-weave linen, and threads of chenille, plastic, wool, cotton and linen have been used. Beads and sequins of plastic, glass and metal have been incorporated. The background colour is cream, the applied felts are red and blue whilst threads and beads include yellow, orange, blue and green. The technique has been restricted to hand embroidery and a wide range of stitches have been used including couching, eyelets, woven webs, french knots, chain stitches and beading.

Other works by Jean Carter are illustrated on pages 34–38.

And the Darkness He called Night/by Wendy Lees
Embroidery

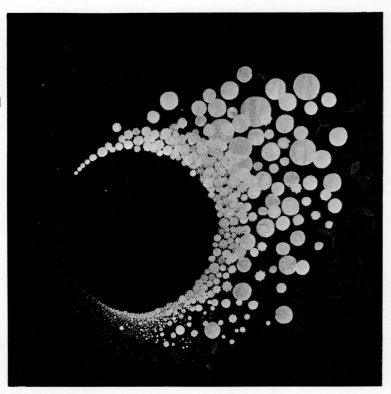

An accident—the spilling of talcum powder upon a black floor—was the inspiration for this large embroidered hanging by Wendy Lees. It measures about 4 feet 6 inches square. The area covered by the talcum powder measured about $4\frac{1}{2}$ inches across and when a small stool was lifted from the spot a clear black circle was left.

The artist kept the black and white colour scheme. Circles of net, Crimplene, rayon and woollen tweed have been applied to a black woollen background. The applied fabrics vary from white to cream. They explode from a solid velvety arc and appear to oscillate.

The work is enriched by embroidered woven webs executed in many types of white thread. Some are raised over a bead or wooden button mould, some are built on top of others. The ensuing richness is accentuated by the addition of sequins and beads and a rich encrusted effect achieved.

Wendy Lees did not at first give the work a title, but the idea of Night from the Creation seemed apt. It did in fact stimulate a second panel entitled '. . . and the Light He called Day' in which a similar design was worked in glowing colours upon a white ground.

Cross and Crown of Thorns/by Janet Warner   Embroidery

This work appears in full colour
opposite page 49.

'Cross and Crown of Thorns' is a
pulpit fall by Janet Warner. The
design originated from drawings made
of a cross section of a dried fruit. The
drawings were developed into a
cruciform shape with symbolic thorns
and nails added.

The pulpit fall has been executed in red
felts and gold kid on an even-weave
rayon background of dark purple. Red
and gold threads give added richness.

The artist is greatly influenced by all
aspects of natural form and this has
inspired much of her work. Ideas
frequently originate from her black and
white drawings; these are then developed
in fabric and thread. Shapes and lines
are amended in the process and the
finished work often differs from the
first idea.

Symbols/by Tadek Beutlich   *Tapestry*

An unusual tapestry technique has been
employed by Tadek Beutlich for
'Symbols'. Strips about 1 inch wide
were woven first with warp of linen
and weft of wool. These strips were
then used as a warp for the whole
work, the weft being of fine linen.
Colours are dramatic reds and blues,
the result a powerful hanging some
8 feet square.

Details of other hangings by Tadek
Beautlich are to be found on pages
67–68 and 80–81.

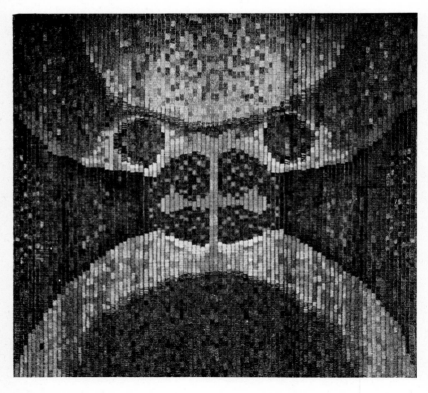

And the earth brought forth grass and herb yielding seed/ by Eleanor Scarfe   Tapestry

This tapestry approximately 40 inches by 52 inches, 'And the earth brought forth grass and herb yielding seed' is more representational than others by Eleanor Scarfe. The idea came as a result of using a close-up lens on her camera. When looking at a summer meadow, the near buttercups stood out in sharp focus, the remaining scene melted into a textured blur.

In weaving the work the artist kept more or less to natural colours, but the tactile nature of the woven threads has a special quality and a tapestry of brilliant colour resulted.

Other tapestries by Eleanor Scarfe are illustrated on pages 69–71.

Win Evans' early work in calligraphy, wood engraving and metalwork involved her in line and shape. A growing interest in colour and the use of dyes resulted in a concern for all aspects of the use of fabric and thread.

The woven hanging 'Trine' uses the basic 'summer and winter' threading which gives a mathematically proportioned basis for an essay in colour. To this is added an extra 'wandering warp' giving a three-dimensional effect.

Woven mainly in wool, there is some mercerized cotton and fibre to give a contrasting sheen. Reds and blues predominate with the 'wandering warp' in gold.

The idea for 'Trine' developed as the artist contemplated the Trinity—the grouping of the three—the union of Father, Son and Holy Ghost, in one Godhead.

Details of another weaving by Win Evans are to be found on page 84.

Laudian Throwover/by Theo Moorman

The Laudian Throwover illustrated was commissioned for the nave altar in Manchester Cathedral in 1969. The altar measures 8 feet by 2 feet by 36½ inches.

The interior of the sombre 16th century building seemed to need a strong focal point of colour and light. The throwover which completely covers the free standing nave altar was designed to meet this need. It is woven in wool and other materials including metallics in an inlay technique which has been developed by Theo Moorman over a number of years.

The basic colour is flame. The rock shapes inspired by the Pembrokeshire coast are in greys, white and silver. Heavy textured effects have been introduced to enhance the dramatic effect. Theo Moorman's wish was to convey the idea of strength and joy.

Works in Public and Private Collections

The following lists refer to hangings illustrated in this book. The artists have, of course, many other works in various collections.

Public Collections

Orange Band Anne Butler
Kent County Council

Sunny Summer Flowers Jean Carter
Kirkby Fields College of Education
Kirkby, Near Liverpool

Dawn Joy Clucas
Homerton College, Cambridge

Warrior Rosalind Floyd
Victoria and Albert Museum, London

Hanging with Coil David Holbourne
Aberdeen City Art Gallery

Asteroid Anne Maile
County of Reading Education
Committee

Imagination Anne Maile
Leicestershire County Council

Laudian Throwover Theo Moorman
Manchester Cathedral

The Downs Heather Padfield
Hertfordshire County Council

Rush Hour Vera Sherman
Nottinghamshire County Council,
Education Committee

Tranquil Yellow Janet Warner
University of Durham, Trevelyan
College

Private

Wall Hanging Tadek Beutlich
Talisman Tadek Beutlich
In Blue Anne Butler
Direction Anne Butler
Orchid (in U.S.A.) Jean Campbell
Rock Pools Jean Carter
Wilting Moonflower Jean Carter
Magic Flower Jean Carter
Glimpse of Golden Fields (in U.S.A.)
  Jean Carter
Fireworks Joy Clucas
Fantasy Joy Clucas
Solar Night Joy Clucas
Winter Joy Clucas
Corduroy Rug Peter Collingwood
Macrogauze Peter Collingwood
Match Noel Dyrenforth
Sun Rosalind Floyd
Contrasts (in U.S.A.) Myriam Gilby
White Bird Margaret Kaye
In Full Bloom Anne Maile
Scoobi-Doo Olga Moyle
Steeple Cynthia Pearson
Cock and Hen Vera Sherman
This Maddening Crowd (in U.S.A.)
  Vera Sherman
Angry Gander Vera Sherman
Black Beauty Eirian Short
Mexican Sun Eirian Short
Nasturtium Audrey Tucker

Part Three—The Artists

Biographical Notes

Beryl Ash

Born in Rugby. Studied at University of Birmingham 1945–51. Obtained Diploma in Psychology of Childhood. Later trained at Bourneville School of Art, Birmingham. Currently Principal Lecturer in Art at the Froebel Institute, Roehampton. Co-author of *Introducing Dyeing and Printing* (Batsford).

Ellen Beutlich

Born 1930. Studied at Camberwell School of Art. Awarded National Diploma in Design, 1955 (specializing in hand weaving and embroidery). Taught adult students in Colleges of Further Education, now works freelance. Works in collections of Education Committees.

Tadek Beutlich

Born in Lwowek, Poland. Studied art in Poland, Italy and England. One-man shows of Tapestries and Prints at Grabowski Gallery, London, and Arras Gallery, New York. Mixed exhibitions in England, Europe, U.S.A., Australia and Japan. Took part in 3rd and 4th Biennale Internationale de la Tapisserie, Lausanne, Switzerland, 1967 and 1969; Modern British Hangings, Edinburgh 1970. Exhibited at University of California 1971. Executed many commissions, most recent being tapestries for University of Southampton and Civic Centre, Castleford. Author of *The Technique of Woven Tapestry* (Batsford).

Richard Box

Born Brighton, Sussex, 1943. Studied painting at Goldsmiths' School of Art 1960–65. Obtained N.D.D. and A.T.C. Now Lecturer in painting at Avery Hill College. One-man shows in U.K. Mixed exhibitions in England and abroad. Works in public and private collections.

Anne Butler

Is Head of Embroidery, Manchester College of Art and Design. Has written *Teaching Children Embroidery* (Studio Vista) and *Simple Stitches* (Batsford). Co-author of *Embroidery in the Primary School*. Has undertaken work for architects and ecclesiastical authorities. Has exhibited widely. Represented in the Biennale de la Tapisserie, Lausanne, Switzerland, 1971. Works in private and public collections in Great Britain and Australia.

Jean Campbell

Born 1947 at Newcastle on Tyne. Trained at Hull College of Art and Manchester College of Art and Design. Awarded Dip.A.D. and Certificate of Education. Work purchased by Education Authorities and private collectors in Great Britain and U.S.A. Currently working freelance.

Jean Carter
Born Oxted, Surrey, 1930. Trained
Tunbridge Wells School of Art and
Regional College of Art, Manchester.
Awarded N.D.D. in Embroidery
and Printed Textiles. A.T.C.,
A.T.D.(Manc). Now Lecturer in
Embroidery at Eastbourne College of
Education. Member of 62 Group.
Lectures and exhibits widely. Her
work is in collections of Education
Authorities, Public Galleries and private
collectors in England, Australia and
U.S.A. Has written *Creative Play with
Fabrics and Threads* (Batsford).

Joy Clucas
Studied art and crafts at Southampton,
Bromley and Brighton Colleges of
Art. Lectures and exhibits widely. Has
been represented in exhibitions in
Great Britain, New Zealand, Australia
and South Africa. Has work in private
collections and in collections of
Education Authorities and Public
Galleries in these countries and in the
U.S.A. Two works from the
Contemporary Hangings purchased by
the Victoria and Albert Museum.

Peter Collingwood
Born 1922. Qualified as doctor. Gave
up medicine and started weaving
workshop 1950. Has exhibited
internationally and is represented in
public and private collections in
England, U.S.A., Europe and
Australia. Numerous commissions for
architects, including rugs for New
Zealand House, tapestries for Shell
Tower and York University, wall
hangings for Selwyn College,

Cambridge. Two-man show, with the
potter Hans Coper, at the Victoria
and Albert Museum 1969. Author of
The Techniques of Rug Weaving
(Faber & Faber).

Noel Dyrenforth
Born 1936 in London. Studied drawing
and painting. Has exhibited batik
widely. Five one-man shows in the
United Kingdom. Mixed exhibitions
in Europe, U.S.A. and Japan.
Represented in public collections
including Victoria and Albert Museum,
Greater London Council and Bradford
City Art Gallery. Works in many
County Education Committee
collections.

Win Evans
Born at Solihull, Warwickshire.
Educated at King's High School,
Warwick. Trained at Birmingham
College of Art. Latterly was teaching
at Redruth School of Art, Cornwall.
Now Senior Lecturer in Textiles at
Christ Church College, Canterbury.
Her work has been exhibited at the
Victoria and Albert Museum, the
Design Centre, the Commonwealth
Institute and at the Bear Lane Gallery,
Oxford. Has exhibited with the Devon
Guild of Craftsmen in New York and
represented in Modern British Hangings
Edinburgh 1970.

Rosalind Floyd
Studied Art and Crafts at Mansfield
School of Art and Leicester College of
Art. Currently lecturing at Rachel
McMillan College of Education,
London. Has exhibited widely, her

work being purchased by private collectors and Education Authorities. The Victoria and Albert Museum purchased a work from the London showing of the Contemporary Hangings exhibition.

Myriam Gilby
Born in South India. Studied Art at Regent Street Polytechnic. Obtained N.D.D. in Sculpture 1951, Art Teachers' Diploma at Goldsmiths' College in 1952. Currently teaching in Loughton, Essex. Her wall hangings and paintings have been exhibited widely and are in private collections in England and U.S.A. Represented in Modern British Hangings, Edinburgh 1970. Member of London Guild of Weavers and World Crafts Council.

Janet Graham
Born 1932 at Luton, Bedfordshire. Studied at Goldsmiths' College. Has wide teaching experience. Currently lecturing at Rachel McMillan College of Education, London. Exhibits with the 62 Group and Designer Craftsmen. Various commissions for the Church of England including a Cope and Mitre for the Bishop of London.

Jennifer Gray
Studied from 1949–53 at Ravensbourne College of Art and Design, specializing in hand embroidery. Teacher training at Brighton College of Art 1954. Appointed to teach hand and machine embroidery at Hull College of Art and Crafts. Has shown at the Commonwealth Institute, the Victoria and Albert Museum and with the Yorkshire artists and the 62 Group. Commissions include work for architects and ecclesiastical authorities. Designed hassocks and kneelers for Girton College chapel.

David Holbourne
Born 1944 in London. Worked for two years in display studio before studying painting and tapestry weaving. Later specialized in tapestry weaving and made first sculptures using textile materials and techniques. Contributed to mixed exhibitions in England and U.S.A. Invited to exhibition of Crafts in Tokyo 1969, Modern British Hangings in Edinburgh 1970. Visiting Lecturer at Winchester School of Art.

Ruth Hurle
At 14 accepted as the youngest female at the Royal Academy Painting School. Awarded Academy 5 Year Diploma and Leverhulme Grant. Has exhibited as a member of the Red Rose Guild and Designer-Craftsmen. Has had one-man show at the Crafts Centre and participated in group exhibitions touring Australia, Europe and Great Britain. Represented in Modern British Hangings, Edinburgh 1970. Teaches weaving at Stanhope Institute and takes instruction courses in weaving for the handicapped.

Margaret Kaye
Studied stained glass work at Croydon School of Art and the Royal College of Art and at present is teaching at the Camberwell School of Art. Her work has been purchased by many leading galleries, including the Victoria and

Albert Museum. Has had six one-man shows at Roland, Browse and Delbanco, London, and executed commissions for ecclesiastical authorities and shipping lines. Married to stage designer and art director, Reece Pemberton.

Wendy Lees

Born in Cirencester. Obtained A.T.D. at Leeds College of Art, specializing in lithography and printmaking. Has taught at Mid Warwickshire School of Art and was art therapist at Central Hospital, Warwick. Currently teaching embroidery at Hampton School of Needlework. Lectures at Adult Education Centres. Exhibits with Designer-Craftsmen and Embroiderers' Guild. Works are in collections of schools and colleges.

Anne Maile

Trained at Leicester College of Art, and Camberwell School of Art. A Fellow of the Society of Designer-Craftsmen and a member of the Crafts Council of Great Britain and the Craft Centre of Great Britain. She is a well-known lecturer and is widely represented in public and private collections. Her book *Tie and Dye as a Present Day Craft* (Mills & Boon) has recently been reprinted and translated into German, Dutch, French and Spanish. Her latest publication is *Tie and Dye Made Easy*, also from Mills & Boon.

Theo Moorman

Born Leeds. Studied at Central School of Art, London. Has worked as industrial fabric designer and hand weaver. For over ten years, Assistant Regional Director, Arts Council, Yorkshire Region. Now specializing in weaving of tapestries and wall hangings. Works commissioned or purchased by Cathedrals of Gloucester, Wakefield, Manchester and Ripon and by colleges, churches and schools throughout the country. Represented in private and public collections in Great Britain and U.S.A. Lectures regularly in U.S.A.

Olga Moyle

Trained at Leeds College of Art as a lithographer and is now Head of the School of Art and Design at Kidderminster and mainly concerned with the design and production of carpets. She has held three one-man shows and contributed to travelling exhibitions. Has sold a group of paintings to I.C.I. and has work in private collections in U.S.A., Italy and France.

Cecil O'Donohue

Is an Associate (Diploma in Design) of the National College of Art, Dublin and is on the textile staff of the college. Her work has been shown in Embroiderers' Guild exhibitions and at the Ecclesiastical Embroidery Exhibition, St. Paul's Cathedral 1968. She is represented in collections in England and Ireland.

Heather Padfield

Born Peterborough 1941. Lives in London. Studied at Goldsmiths' College School of Art 1960–64.

Works purchased by London, Brighton, Reading, Leicester, Sussex, Hertford and Wolverhampton Education Authorities. Represented in many private collections in England, Guernsey and France. Has shown with the travelling exhibitions of the Victoria and Albert Museum, 62 Group and Smithsonian Institution. Now teaches at Coloma College of Education, West Wickham, Kent.

Cynthia Pearson
Born 1939. Trained in printed and woven textiles at Stourbridge College of Art. Lecturer in Embroidery at School of Art, Kidderminster College of Further Education. One-man Exhibition, Birmingham 1968. Works in Collections of Viking Sewing Machine Co., and in other private collections.

Christine Risley
Studied painting at Goldsmiths' College. Obtained N.D.D. in Painting. Taught design and machine embroidery at St. Martin's School of Art. Currently Lecturer in Machine Embroidery at Goldsmiths' College. Has published *Machine Embroidery* and *Creative Embroidery* (Studio Vista). Exhibited at the Hanover Gallery and in the English, Welsh and Scottish 'Pictures for Schools' exhibitions, in the Arts Council travelling exhibitions, with the Society of Designer Craftsmen in Yugoslavia and in galleries all over England. Has sold to many Education Committees, the I.L.E.A. and to private collectors.

Barbara Sawyer
Trained at Birmingham College of Art and Manchester College of Technology. Currently Lecturer in Weaving at Camberwell School of Art. Designer in textiles. Member of Society of Designer-Craftsmen, Red Rose Guild and Crafts Centre of Great Britain. Has exhibited at centres in Great Britain, Ireland, Canada and U.S.A. Represented in Modern British Hangings, Edinburgh 1970.

Eleanor Scarfe
Studied drawing and painting at Brighton College of Art. Awarded Art Teachers Diploma. Visiting Lecturer at the Regent Street Polytechnic (1951–61); Goldsmiths' College (1959–64) in drawing and tapestry weaving. At present Senior Lecturer in Art and Crafts at Coloma College of Education. Exhibited in London and Provincial Galleries, including the Victoria and Albert Museum, Whitechapel Gallery and Royal Academy. Works purchased by Education Authorities and private collectors in London, New York, Paris, Vienna and Johannesburg. Married to Laurence Scarfe, A.R.C.A., F.S.I.A.

Vera Sherman
Trained in London at the Regent Street Polytechnic, obtaining the National Diploma in Design for Painting. Later took a Post-Graduate Course in Sculpture. In 1964 awarded the Premio Internazionale Europa Arte award for extensive and meritorious artistic activities. Works in collections

of Public Galleries, Education
Authorities and private collectors in
Great Britain, Australia, Lebanon,
Portugal, Spain, Sweden, Turkey and
U.S.A. Organizer of the touring
exhibitions 'Contemporary Hangings'
and 'Contemporary Pictures in Fabric
and Thread'.

Eirian Short
Born Wales 1924. After the war
studied sculpture, then embroidery, at
Goldsmiths' School of Art. From 1951
exhibited embroidery and collages at
Pictures for Schools, Crafts Centre,
Embroiderers' Guild and in public
and private galleries. Works sold to
Education Authorities, National
Museum of Wales, business firms and
private buyers. Author of *Embroidery
and Fabric Collage* (Pitman) and
Introducing Macramé (Batsford).
Lectures widely. Freelance designer
for collage and embroidery. Married
to painter Denys Short.

Gabriel Sitkey
Born in Budapest, Hungary. Won
scholarship to Academy of Applied
Arts where he stayed until the
Hungarian Revolution of 1956. Came
to England, was encouraged by Linda
Youngman and influenced by Michael
Rothenstein. In Paris was influenced
by William Hayter who taught him
printmaking. Has travelled in Europe,
Greece, the Middle East and U.S.A.
Lecturer and designer of textiles. Most
of his batik works are in private
collections.

Audrey Tucker
Born Barnstaple 1940. Studied Bideford
and Hammersmith Colleges of Art.
Awarded N.D.D. in Hand and
Machine Embroidery. Seven years'
teaching and lecturing experience with
G.L.C. and Loughborough College of
Art. Now works freelance.
Exhibits widely. Works purchased by
Education Authorities and private
collectors. Ecclesiastical commissions
include hanging for St. Anselm's
Chapel, Manchester University.

Janet Warner
Born Skipton, Yorkshire, 1944. Studied
printed textiles at Leicester College of
Art and Design. Gained Diploma in
Art and Design and Art Teachers
Diploma. Divides time between
teaching and freelance work. Has
exhibited with the Crafts Council of
Great Britain, the Midland Group and
in centres throughout the country.
Three one-man shows. Has undertaken
ecclesiastical commissions and sold to
industry, Education Authorities and
private collectors.